FACE AT THE BOTTOM OF THE WORLD
and Other Poems

BY HAGIWARA SAKUTARŌ

FACE AT THE BOTTOM OF THE WORLD

OF THE WORLD
and Other Poems

BY HAGIWARA SAKUTARŌ

translated by GRAEME WILSON
paintings by YORK WILSON

York Wilson

CHARLES E. TUTTLE COMPANY
Rutland · Vermont : Tokyo · Japan

Representatives

For Continental Europe:
BOXERBOOKS, INC., *Zurich*

For the British Isles:
PRENTICE-HALL INTERNATIONAL, INC., *London*

For Australasia:
PAUL FLESCH & CO., PTY. LTD., *Melbourne*

For Canada:
M. G. HURTIG LTD., *Edmonton*

UNESCO COLLECTION OF REPRESENTATIVE WORKS: JAPANESE
SERIES. This book has been accepted in the Japanese Series of
the Translation Collection of the United Nations Educational,
Scientific and Cultural Organization (UNESCO).

*Published by the Charles E. Tuttle Company, Inc.
of Rutland, Vermont & Tokyo, Japan
with editorial offices at Suido 1-chome, 2-6, Bunkyo-ku, Tokyo*

*©1969 by Charles E. Tuttle Co., Inc.
All rights reserved*

*Library of Congress Catalog Card No. 75-83075
Standard Book No. 8048 0176-2*

First printing, 1969

Book design & typography by F. Sakade
PRINTED IN JAPAN

For
MAYUMI

TABLE OF CONTENTS

ACKNOWLEDGMENTS

Acknowledgments are made to the editors of the following publications in which various of these translations have appeared: the *Japan Quarterly*, the *Oriental Economist*, the *P.E.N. Review of Japan*, the *East-West Review*, the *Times Literary Supplement*, the *Spectator*, the *Observer*, the *New Statesman & Nation*, the *Cornhill Magazine*, *Encounter*, *Tablet*, *English*, *Tribune*, the *Poetry Review*, the *Glasgow Herald*, the *Scotsman*, *New Nation*, *Chirimo*, *Solidaridad*, the *Diliman Review*, *Enquiry*, *Poetry Singapore*, the *Bangkok Magazine*, *Poetry Australia*, the *Poetry Magazine*, the *Meanjin Quarterly*, *Twentieth Century*, *Poetry India*, the *Weekend Review*, *Now*, *Mainstream*, *Quest*, *Thought*, *Edge*, *Prism International*, *Delos*, *New* and the *Yale Review*.

INTRODUCTION

The poetry of Hagiwara Sakutarō is still little known in the English-speaking world, though this is not altogether surprising when the importance of his work remains inadequately recognized in Japan itself. Nearly all Japanese critiques of post-Meiji poetry acknowledge Hagiwara as one of the best (if not, indeed, the very best) of modern Japanese poets; but almost all critics, having briefly made some such admission, thereafter shy away from him, strangely to devote long paragraphs to other poets patently less talented, sadly more diffuse and far less influential. Why? Perhaps the reason is that Hagiwara, for all his brilliance, seems somehow to switch on darkness, to radiate black luminance. In the beaconry of modern Japanese literature he is an occulting, rather than a flashing, light: but he remains nevertheless a lighthouse of supreme importance.

*   *   *

Hagiwara was born on November 1st 1886 at Maebashi, a provincial town near Tokyo where his father was a successful doctor, initially in government service and later in private practice. The family was typical of the new Japanese middle class deliberately created by the policy-makers of the Meiji regime, and his home environment was characterized by its openness to then-modern influences: electric light, the magic lantern, ping-pong, western chairs and tables, summer holidays at the seaside, western playing-cards, the piano, the guitar, the mouth-organ. The eldest of six children, he was a sickly and hence a spoilt child, remaining his mother's lifelong darling. An unsatisfactory student, his failure to achieve the academic distinction of which he was obviously capable reflected as much a lazy man's unwillingness as a sick man's inability to concentrate. He neither went to a University nor ever seriously studied to develop his natural talent for music. Indeed, modern critics conscious of his proven genius show an under-standable reluctance to say flatly whether some of the curious words in his poetry are deliberate new-coinings or merely results of his lack of formal education. On leaving school, he drifted into a vaguely Bohemian life and spent the years 1910–13 oscillating between Mae-bashi and Tokyo, reading, learning to play the mando-lin, listening to opera, attending foreign plays, reviewing Kabuki performances, writing poetry. His father's dis-appointment was more than matched by the disapproval of his beatnik behavior evinced by the respectable bour-geoisie of Maebashi; and Hagiwara's poetry is full of acid and even vengeful references to his native place and its inhabitants.

His early poetry is all apprentice stuff in the traditional

tanka form of five lines of 5:7:5:7:7 syllables. Never-theless, by 1913 he had won a more than modest reputa-tion as a new poet in that traditional mode, and had already decided to devote his life to literature. He formed useful friendships in the literary world; espe-cially those with the then already well-established poets Yosano Akiko (1878–1942) and Kitahara Hakushū (1885–1943), and with two other excellent rising poets Murō Saisei (1889–1962) and Yamamura Bochō (1884–1924). Then, suddenly, in 1913, he began writing those astonishing and essentially modern poems on which his real and lasting reputation rests. His first book, *Tsuki ni Hoeru* (Barking at the Moon) appeared in 1917. It made an immediate impact, involved a brush with the Imperial Censor over the allegedly corrupting influence on the young of two of its poems *(Person Who Loves Love* and *Ai Ren),* and is still widely regarded as his most characteristic work. The rest of his life, in which, despite quick recognition as a leading contemporary writer, he largely depended for financial support upon his father, was devoted to producing a stream of books: six volumes of poetry, several of criticism, two major studies of poetic theory, a novel, an extremely influ-ential study of Buson, and a flood of prose-poems, aphorisms, essays, articles, radio-scripts and miscella-neous writings.

In 1919 he married Ueda Ineko but, though two daughters were born (Yōko in 1920 and Akiko in 1922), the marriage was a failure and ended in 1929. A second marriage in 1938 to Ōya Mitsuko proved equally luck-less, and she left him in eighteen months. The loneliness, nihilism and desperation of his later life are painfully reflected in his poems, and the posthumous account of him written by his daughter Yōko paints a poignant picture of the aging poet, fascinated by stage-magic and simple conjuring tricks, drifting into alienation and a persistent drunkenness. Kitahara Hakushū, in his introduction to *Barking at the Moon,* had likened the quality in Hagiwara's early poetry to that of a "razor soaked in gloomy scent", to the "flash of a razor in a bowl of cool mercury". The razor-edge was never seriously blunted, but its scent soured into the smell of stale beer; and Murō, in his poem on Hagiwara's death, significantly referred to the phenomena of continuing life as "for you mere *saké* spilt along the bar". Hagiwara himself explained his especial liking for beer as permitting long arguments about poetry as one proceeded slowly toward incoherence. Miyoshi Tatsuji, Japan's best poet between Hagiwara's death in 1942 and his own in 1964, has described long fascinating discussions with Hagiwara as he sat drinking steadily in his favorite corner of his favorite beer-hall in Shinjuku; but it is Hagiwara, and Hagiwara only, whom Miyoshi recognizes as his master. The poet's lonely life was lightened by a variety of new literary friendships; and the deepest (that with Miyoshi) lasted happily, save for some acrimony over the latter's frank confession of his dislike of Hagiwara's last book of poems *(The Ice Land* of 1934), until the poet's death of pneumonia on May 11th 1942.

* * *

Hagiwara began writing during that critical period

in the history of Japanese literature when western in-fluences, almost overwhelming in the Meiji Era (1868–1912), were at last being so successfully assimilated as to permit the re-growth of that essentially Japanese spirit which characterized the succeeding Taisho Era (1912–26). By 1910 the seeds dropped from foreign flowers, not all of them *Fleurs du Mal,* into the loam of Japanese consciousness were coming up like cryptomeria. *Wakon yōsai,* that Meiji slogan stressing the need to meld "western learning and the Japanese spirit", was still a living inspiration; and Hagiwara, working in full aware-ness thereof, achieved universality.

It is still sometimes said that the artist's function is to hold a mirror up to nature. The time when that remark was true, if ever such a time there was, is now long past. The photographers have taken over; the photographers who implement the lawyers' pettifogging mania for reasonable facsimiles. The artist's function is (and has, I fancy, always been) to hold up mirrors that transmit not the photographers' literal reality but the artist's in-dividual, even his cracked, perception of the universe. His function in the world is, I believe, to create un-reasonable facsimiles thereof. For artists, especially lyric poets such as Hagiwara, are not concerned with truths verifiable by photographs, by the due processes of the law, or by the disciplines of formal logic. They have those reasons reason does not know. Hagiwara was once asked to explain the meaning of an early poem. He replied by asking if his questioner considered beautiful the nightingale's song. On receiving the inevitable af-firmative, he then asked what that bird-song meant. . . .

[15]

For Hagiwara holds no mirror, cracked or common-place, up to nature: mirrors need light. Instead, he turns a radar onto nature's hitherto unpenetrated darknesses, feeling out shapes invisible. The resultant images, shining, golden or greeny-silver, often indeed distorted, may, to a photographer's eye, seem odd; but they are authentic versions, visions even, of the truth. For Hagiwara was a native of that strange world where Dylan Thomas' question ("Isn't life a terrible thing, thank God") really needs no answer. And of that world his poems are a terrible, but a beautiful, reporting.

Hagiwara's earliest truly modern poems, of which the first examples appeared in magazines during 1913, show traces of the influence of Baudelaire and the French Symbolists. He has, in fact, been called "the Japanese Baudelaire" but, though there are obvious resemblances in their attitudes, Hagiwara's poetry (as distinct from his prose) contains none of the intellectualism of his predecessor. Similarly, those poems in which he shows most resemblance to Rimbaud are in the lighter lyrical field; and it is interesting to compare Hagiwara's *Elegant Appetite* with Rimbaud's *Au Cabaret Vert,* the latter the poem in which Ezra Pound considers Rimbaud's real originality to be found. Though Hagiwara's work rings with a certain natural pessimism and despair (themselves reflections of ill health, ill nerves and plain ill-luck), its tone was deepened by study of Nietzsche, Bergson and Schopenhauer. Not only his first book but also his middle-period poetry (notably the poems in *To Dream of a Butterfly* of 1923 and *Blue Cat* of the same year) exhibit that pure but desperate lyricism which German critics have called "the Keats' sickness". These poems do not argue: they sing. They are, in Japanese, songs of those very nightingales which, in T. S. Eliot's poem,

> "Sang within the bloody wood
> When Agamemnon cried aloud
> And let their liquid siftings fall
> To stain the stiff dishonoured shroud."

As Hagiwara aged, his poetry began to lose its lyrical purity and, though it never sank to the level of logical argument, it did begin to organize its imagery into a sort of argument by visual analogy. At the same time he reverted to a more frequent use of the classical Japanese literary vocabulary (a vocabulary or, to be more precise, a syllabary derived from the Chinese), and his poems so acquired a clanging rather than a singing quality. These stylistic changes, of which *Late Autumn* is a good example, have been praised as marking Hagiwara's development, albeit belatedly, towards a more masculine manner. Such may indeed have been the poet's own intention, but I share Miyoshi's view that the change was a retrogression. I would not go so far as to echo that comment ("Even the powerful bow weakens in the end") which so annoyed Hagiwara, but there can be no doubt that his later poetry contains intellectual elements which adulterate, if they do not actually sour, his earlier pure lyricism. His prose writings demonstrate his reasoned (and, I think, rightly reasoned) antipathy to the styles of political poetry which, almost world wide, characterized the schools of the 1930s; but so far as these poets were poets and not political theorists or would-be politicians, Hagiwara shared their ever-deepening sense of anger, sadness and despair. Some of his later poems such as *Useless Book* and *What I Don't Have Is Everything* are almost querulous. He became eventually so bankrupt of all hope that, in Auden's terrifying words (which might well have been his own), he moved towards the ultimate silence of death

> "Saying Alas
> To less and less."

*   *   *

The reasons for Hagiwara's importance in the history of modern Japanese literature (and, indeed, in the whole history of Japanese literature) may be summarized under the following six headings: his use of novel forms, his use of novel language, his escape from the bonds of traditional metric rhythms, his entirely personal music, his astonishing personal vision, and his unprecedented achievement of sustained lyricism.

The earliest collection of Japanese poetry (the *Man-yōshū* of 759) consists largely of *tanka,* but it also contains many poems in the longer forms of the *chōka* and *sedōka.* However, by the time that Ki no Tsurayuki wrote his catalytic Preface to the *Kokinshū* (the First Imperial Anthology of 905), the Japanese poetic tradition had already begun to crystallize into a tradition of pure lyricism. "Poetry", wrote Tsurayuki, "has its seeds in man's heart"; and this view of poetry as lyricism necessitating no breadth of learning in the lyricist has remained the main strand of the Japanese poetic tradition.

Such a tradition demands precisely that intensity of feeling which is always most tellingly expressed in short forms; and for this reason the *chōka* and *sedōka* withered away. Though at various times in the subsequent development of Japanese poetry, poets struggled for the freedom of such other longer forms as the *imayō, kouta, dodoitsu* and *jōruri,* the five-line *tanka* remained the normal mode of expression. Some measure of freedom appeared to be offered by the development of linked verse *(renga)* in which often different poets would compose successive three-line and two-line groups: but, in the event, this breaking of the *tanka* into a three-line upper hemistich *(kami no ku)* of 5:7:5 syllables and a two-line lower hemistich *(shimo no ku)* of 7:7 syllables merely resulted in a yet greater compression of Japanese poetic form. For the upper hemistich embarked on an independent development to become that flower of Edo poetry, now shriveled to a tourist's gaud, the three-line *haiku*. Thus, at the time when contact was re-established with the outside world in 1868, the main tradition of Japanese poetry was rigidly confined within the narrow courses of the *tanka* and the *haiku*. The notion of poetry as a vehicle for intellectual thought, the concept of the poetry of social protest, the didactic element in Chinese poetry; all these had perished with Yamanoue no Okura (660–733) from the Japanese tradition.

The first result in the poetic field of the Meiji re-opening of windows on the west was the appearance in 1882 of *Shintaishi* (New Style Poetry), a collection of translations of early nineteenth century English poems edited by three Professors (significantly of philosophy, botany and sociology) at the University of Tokyo. The Preface sharply attacked the cramping brevity of traditional forms ("How can a consecutive thought be expressed in such tight forms?"); and three further collections (Shimazaki Tōson's *Seedlings* in 1887, Mori Ōgai's *Semblances* in 1889 and Ueda Bin's *Sound of the Tide* in 1905) pursued the same line of attack but broadened the scope of European impact to include French, German and Italian influences. Nevertheless, the main stream of Japanese poetry continued to flow in the form of *tanka* (notably in the work of Yosano Akiko) and Hagiwara himself wrote hundreds of early poems in that form; the first five appeared in his school magazine in 1902 and the last group (influenced by Kitahara's work in that mode) in 1913. Thus, when in 1913 Hagiwara began to write poems in all manner of irregular and typically "modern" forms, he was by no means the first to abandon traditional Japanese practice, but he was undoubtedly the first Japanese poet successfully to exploit the innovations of form derived from western examples for the expression of traditional Japanese lyricism. It is perhaps worth noting here that Hagiwara did not at any time follow western example into those striking departures from the Japanese lyric tradition which, picking up the didactic tradition where Okura had left it in the eighth century, eventually developed into modern Japanese proletarian poetry and those contemporary schools which, though named after Eliot's early lyrics, in fact derive from his later (and very un-Japanese) "thinking poetry".

[20]

Similarly, though Buson (1716–83) had tentatively experimented with the use of the spoken colloquial language *(kōgotai),* it was not until the Shintaishi movement was very well developed that any serious attempt was made to break away from the literary language derived from Chinese models *(bungotai)* in which *tanka* and *haiku* were traditionally written. The three Tokyo Professors expressed in their Preface "regret that poetry has not hitherto been written in the colloquial language", but the language used to express the subsequent flow of imitations of European poets did little to assuage that sorrow. It was almost certainly Murō Saisei who first fully realized that the future of Japanese poetry lay in the use of *kōgotai* but, especially after Murō turned to the writing of novels, it was left for Hagiwara to exploit that realization and so to become the true father of modern Japanese poetry. Hagiwara exploited the rich resources of the colloquial right down to the darker levels of the vernacular; his claim that "all new poetic styles issued from this book" *(Barking at the Moon)* is, I think, a fair one.

Though the *Manyōshū* contained poems with lines of a notably irregular syllable-count, all subsequent Japanese poetry was constructed from patterns of lines of five and seven syllables; the so-called seven-five metric rhythm *(shichi go chō).* The words of the Japanese language are so built up from unaccented syllables all ending in vowels that rhyme has never been used in its poetry. In parenthesis, one might here remark that one of the further peculiarities of Hagiwara's earliest "modern" poems is that some of them do, in fact, appear to rhyme. However, this basic structure of the language has resulted in a prosody very closely linked to syllable-count, and long experience has confirmed the tradition that the *shichi go chō* is the rhythm most natural to the language. None of the poets of the Shintaishi movement, despite their attacks on traditional form and traditional language, made any attempt to break away from this traditional metric rhythm. The first real efforts in that direction were made by Kawaji Ryūkō in his volume of poems *Hakidame* (Rubbish Heap) published in 1908. But again, though Hagiwara was not the pioneer, he was the first Japanese poet since Manyō times successfully to exploit rhythms other than the *shichi go chō*.

It may well be that Hagiwara's success in that exploitation of Ryūkō's pioneering work was a reflection of his almost professional knowledge of music. He was, lifelong, obsessed by music. As early as 1908 he brought home a violin for the school holidays. In 1910 he wrote to one of his class-mates that "I have three possibilities: as a merchant, through medical school or suicide by pistol", but only his somewhat childish (he was then twenty-four) love of dramatizing his feelings of being misunderstood could have led him to omit the very real possibility that he would become a musician. In 1911 he spent some four months learning the mandolin under an Italian teacher, and made his usual ineffective efforts, this time to prepare for the entrance examination to the Ueno Music School. In 1912 he was studying the guitar in Tokyo, and as late as 1914 he was actually teaching the mandolin in a small western-style music-school then recently established in Maebashi. He organized, conducted and played publicly in musical groups. He published criticism both of western music and of the decline of the *samisen,* and in later life even some minor compositions of his own. Though Beethoven was his favorite composer and though Japanese critics have emphasized the symphonic structure of his middle-period poetry (notably that in *Blue Cat*), his poems reveal an essentially melodic interest. In this connection it is perhaps worth suggesting that the poetry of Hagiwara and the poetry of Frederico Garcia Lorca (his almost exact Spanish contemporary) merit comparative study. It has been acutely remarked that, whereas Lorca was obsessed with the terror of envisaged horrors, Hagiwara was transfixed in lasting horror of terrors long arrived. The two poets shared an absorption in greenness ("Here", wrote Hagiwara, "is a little flute whose music is pure green"; "Green, how I love you, green", wrote Lorca). They shared a feeling for loneliness, for rivered landscapes, moonlight and horizons bounded by the barking of dogs. But, above all, they shared a passion for music, for the melodies in struck strings. Though there are, of course, great differences between them (the differences, basically, between the guitar and the mandolin), their high-strung similarities remain. There is no evidence that Hagiwara was aware even of Lorca's existence, and his introduction of an almost western melodic line to Japanese poetry is an entirely original contribution. But it is so real a contribution that some of his poems (notably *Dice of Pure Silver*), if they are ever successfully to be translated out of Japanese, will probably have to go into music.

Hagiwara's most astonishing originality lies, however, in his unique vision of the world. He had, highly developed, the poet's one essential gift: to see first what all can see once it has been shown to them. "Truth", said John Donne, "is a mountain: who would know Truth, about it and about must go". Hagiwara saw that mountain from his own strange belvedere, and his poems remain like arrow-slits in some cold and lonely siege-tower commanding their singular view of the truth. Some have said that his viewpoint was so restricted as to present a topsy-turvy truth, the universe *in camera oscura:* others, that he stood so close to Donne's great mountain that inevitably he stood in shadow. But there seems no dispute that, whatever aspect of the truth he saw, none had quite so clearly studied it before him. It is, I think, irrelevant that Hagiwara revealed so dark a beauty.

> "Who, grown, can look in a true mirror
> And have no horror?"

Hagiwara saw everything (not, perhaps, everyone) afresh, as if new-made, as if in vision. Indeed, I deduce he must have had constant access to that admittedly lowest level of mystical experience, the Vision of Dame Kind. How rarely are his poems concerned with relations other than relations with things (a characteristic of that Vision); and how frequently he uses not only the word "things" but the visionary's key-word "shining". I know no other poet, except perhaps Rimbaud in *Les Illuminations,* so simultaneously lucent and obscure. It is as though Hagiwara knew that the sun, that symbol of Japan, rises as much to cast shadow as to give light. Having abandoned not only traditional forms, traditional language and traditional rhythms but also what little residue of thought lay in the associated traditional stock of ideas, he is sometimes criticized for lack of intellectual content, for failing to react positively to the western revivification of the old Chinese didactic tradition and, in particular, for an uncritical acceptance of the Pathetic Fallacy. But lyric poets are not concerned to maintain logical or philosophical consistencies, and lyricists of Hagiwara's animistic sympathies might well not think that Fallacy fallacious. Though he is buried in the cemetery attached to the Buddhist Shōjun Temple in Maebashi, he seems never to have adopted any specific religion or philosophy, but to have remained a humanistic (or, rather, an animistic) free-thinker all his life. It is, however, relevant to mention, since it explains the otherwise curious frequency of Christian imagery in his poems, that, as a young man, he was much influenced by that cousin, Hagiwara Eiji, a convinced Christian, to whom *Barking at the Moon* is dedicated.

Finally, though Hagiwara stands squarely in the mainstream of the Japanese lyric tradition and though one strand of his poetic ancestry can be traced back through Bashō to that chill and bitter figure, the one-time master-archer of the late twelfth century, Priest Saigyō, he can also claim a place in the main continental European tradition running down through Baudelaire and the

Symbolists to the Imagists and their successors. For the element in Hagiwara's work which is utterly unprecedented in the Japanese poetic tradition is the sheer staying-power of his lyric inspiration, the unexampled length of poem throughout which he was able to sustain an intensity of feeling which, before he wrote, had only been achieved in poems brief as *tanka*. More than for all his other innovations, Hagiwara's chief claim to greatness lies in his unparalleled sustention of lyric intensity. The peculiarly piercing quality of his poetry has been compared to that of a babe new-born into our terrible world. But Hagiwara cried for a lifetime, and in poems that will last as long as the Japanese language.

*   *   *

Contemporary Japanese poets and critics, while acknowledging Hagiwara's primacy, still tend to regard his work as a dead-end. This is, essentially, the criticism made of such slight and minor poets as A. E. Housman; but it seems to me unjustified in respect of Hagiwara. It is argued that the startling originality of his themes and imagery is no more than a direct reflection of the poet's persistent physical ill-health and of his spiritual and intellectual neurasthenia. His poetry's consequent aura of irremediable *malaise,* this argument continues, inevitably appeals to our own distempered times but it disqualifies Hagiwara from a major place in any healthy tradition. Though it can with perfect cogency be answered that all lyric poetry reflects some kind of serious disorder in the lyricist, even an admission of Hagiwara's quintessential sickness seems to me irrelevant to the reasons for the continuing importance of his work. I do not suggest that there would be any merit in contemporary imitation of his individual style, diction, imagery or themes; but I do very strongly suggest that Hagiwara's poetry is almost the only example in modern Japanese literature of the successful integration of the Japanese and western poetic traditions. His poetry is a living synthesis of alien elements, and poets working in either tradition would do well to study the means of his achievement: for Hagiwara has shown that the traditionally compressed Japanese intensity of lyric feeling can be perfectly expressed in the forms and at lengths derived from the western tradition, that the heart of Priest Saigyō can beat in the breast of Lorca. The scientists and surgeons, still baffled by problems of "rejection", struggle along fifty years behind him.

It took Japanese poets some fifty years to absorb the shock of the Meiji admission of western influences, and it may well take another fifty years for the shock sustained in 1945 to be similarly absorbed. The comparative worthlessness, *sub specie aeternitatis,* of the early Meiji imitations of European poets at least suggests the probable worthlessness of contemporary Japanese imitations of the current poetic vogue-styles, themselves not improbably worthless, of the west. There is, of course, no necessary reason why an obsession with the resources of typography, with the re-structuring of established syntax and the theories of Yves Bonnefoy, with Olson's Projective Verse, with Concrete Poetry and with the Intentionalist and Affective Fallacies should result in worthless Japanese poetry; but, in practice, worthlessness appears to result. "Tradition", said Eliot, "is a matter of much wider significance [than novelty]. It cannot be inherited and, if you want it, you must obtain it by great labour. It involves, in the first place, that historical sense nearly indispensable to anyone who would continue a poet beyond his twenty-fifth year. The historical sense compels a man to write not merely with his own generation in his bones, but with a feeling that the whole literature of his own country composes a simultaneous order". In precisely those terms Hagiwara, by enormous labor, established himself in the Japanese tradition. Only those who, like him, can refine and develop the poetic tradition of their own country can hope to become great poets in the future of Japan. Shinoda Hajime has recently expressed the seminal thought that perhaps the similarities between Hagiwara and Eliot reflect their common derivation of essential elements in their work from the main continental European tradition; and, if that thought be accepted, the work of Hagiwara holds lessons not only for Japanese poets of the future but for the future poets of the world. Only time will tell; though I dare in Auden's words to think that "Time will say nothing but I told you so". These matters affect only consideration of Hagiwara's status as a major poet of the world. That he is a major poet of Japan and a poet of as-yet-undetermined world-status cannot, I believe, seriously be challenged. His phenomenal perceptiveness, his lyric hypersensitivity, his remorseless wringing of the nervous system of the soul are unique. And, if in the long run of our tears he does eventually fail to achieve major world-status, it will only be because those very characteristics which give him such laser-sharp penetration necessarily narrow the breadth of his vision. For his, indeed, is the heart-break at the heart of things.

*   *   *

I would add that the forty poems in this book are translations only in the sense that Fitzgerald's *Rubaiyat* is a translation of the work of Omar Khayyam. I have not regarded the literal words in Hagiwara's texts as of prime or even secondary importance. Instead, I have sought first to convey the feel and intent of his work, the meaning of the feelings behind the vocabulary; and, secondly, to re-present those feelings in the forms and vocabulary of English. Cultured Iranians fluent in English sometimes laugh (and so, apparently, does Robert Graves) when told that the English regard Fitzgerald's poem as a translation of the *Rubaiyat*. They are, of course, entitled to their merriment; but I think they miss the point. Fitzgerald knew what he was doing, and he did it well: indeed, it is not impossible (if only because more people understand English than understand the language of the *Rubaiyat*) that Fitzgerald's re-creations will outlast their originals. I make no shadow of any such claim for the durability of my own efforts, for Hagiwara will hold his high position in the world of poetry without need of any alien support. However, I do make claim for the validity of Fitzgerald's mode of translation. Literal translations serve a useful purpose and have their honored place; but they are hall-marked, branded even, by their need for explanatory footnotes. They are, in fact, clay-footnoted. In contrast, works in Fitzgerald's mode, though they be re-creations, remain creations and aspire to life. They have, and need, no footnotes. They explain, because they are, themselves. It follows, of course, that if they fail to come alive they must come to nothing. *"Traduttori traditori"* say the Italians. Translators are traitors. But if these versions of Hagiwara's poetry can in any way foster a reappraisal or a wider recognition of his work, I gladly risk that complete oblivion which is a traitor's fittest doom.

> "Treason never prospers. And the reason?
> That, if it prosper, none dare call it treason."

All such translations are, like parody, a form of criticism. But their intent is not the cold intent of parody, and their criticism goes more deep: it goes, I hope, to the heart. For though translators must in some real sense be traitors, what other form of criticism goes deeper than does treachery?

*   *   *

In conclusion, I should perhaps explain that, lacking Hagiwara's Catullan delicacy of ear, I have, in translating his poetry (which Auden once brilliantly defined as memorable speech), sought to maintain its memorability with all those technical devices, notably of form, which Hagiwara could afford to disregard. Similarly I have exploited rhyme which, since (as discussed above) it moves unhappily in the Japanese language, Hagiwara, who used every other pattern of repeated sound and like-sound, very rarely used. Conventional forms have, I believe, developed and survived into conventionality precisely because they mirror best the nature of the human mind. Diamonds could presumably be cut into the shapes of peacocks, people or pantechnica: but the nature of light and the nature of diamond are, in fact, such that the gem reflects most light when cut in shapes that conform to the realities of nature. Poetry, whose deepest roots go down to incantation and whose strength derives from simple song and dancing, risks a withering the more certain the more it fails to reflect the nature of its sources. Hagiwara, a very great poet, could take that risk. I cannot. But if these translations, these transmutations, open for the English-speaking reader even the thinnest band of Hagiwara's orchestrated multi-colored vision, I shall be as well content as he, *frère hypocrite lecteur,* will be lucky.

*   *   *

The illustrations with which York Wilson has graced this book do not relate to any one particular poem or group of poems. They are, in essence, black-and-white representations of "Hagiwara-ness". Like Hagiwara's poems, they feel out shapes invisible. I have never been able to understand the sharp distinction drawn by modern art-critics between abstract and representational (or figurative) art. To my mind all art is abstract. This notion can easily be verified by asking any group of so-called representational artists to draw or paint the same object. Each such artist will produce a recognizably different version of the object's reality, even though all such representational versions can be immediately recognized as versions of the original object. It would seem to follow that even the most literal representational artist is nevertheless producing abstractions from reality. The so-called abstract artist merely takes the same process further. York Wilson's work has, over the years, in one sense changed from a representational to an increasingly abstract mode; but, in a far more real sense, he has simply developed the depth, the subtlety and the penetration with which he has continuously been engaged in the abstraction of images from reality. The accompanying illustrations are thus graphic versions of those truths for which Hagiwara so long, so painfully and so successfully searched.

*　　　*　　　*

I cannot conclude this Introduction without expressing my thanks to those many friends of all nationalities without whose help this book could never have been written. In particular I would like to record my deep indebtedness to Itō Aiko, to George Saitō, to Hagiwara Yōko and to Atsumi Ikuko. *Memine me salamandrum, non mercatorem.*

GRAEME WILSON

Hong Kong

HAGIWARA SAKUTARŌ

蘇軾職太原

秋原朔太郎

THE POEMS

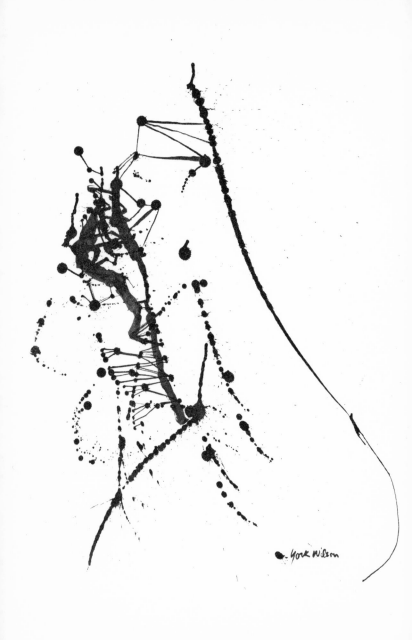

愛
憐 *AI REN*

O surely with your sweet hard teeth
Woman, my otherness, you
Will chew the green stem of the grass
That, with its faintly blue
Ink, I may so paint your face
Here where the grass grows dense
That your slow heart's intensities
May grow the more intense.

Look, here's a dotted bell-flower
That shakes a hanging head,
And here the gentian's little hand
Moves languid on its bed.

Hard as I hug your breasts, your body
Hard-presses mine that we
May squeeze from this abandoned place
Our snaking ecstasy;
And, as I love you piercingly,
I'll stain your stainless skin
With ooze from blue bruised grasses
Such juiciness was in.

緑色の笛 *GREEN FLUTE*

Over the evening field
The elephants, long-eared,
Troop slowly into night.

The yellow evening moon
Limps up from afternoon
To stand at last revealed
Clear yellow but yet bleared
By waverings, the slight
Wind-winnowing of the light.

Girl in this evening scene,
Are you not saddened by
Its seep of loneliness?

Here is a little flute
Whose music is pure green.
Blow on it gently, sigh
Along its hollows. See,
Its quavered cadences,
Its shaky melody,
Call down from that clear sky
A cold, an absolute
Quintessence of distress.

From some far sea of yearning
A ghostliness appears.

With slow appalling pad
It lurks towards us, turning
More nasty as it nears,
Seeming at last to be
A cat without a head
That staggers in the dead
Black shadows of this sad
Unseemly cemetery.

Girl, I could easily
In such a place concerning
Grief and the end of day,
Grief and the night returning,
To death's menagerie
Stagger away.

 DUEL

Both earth and sky are greennesses,
Greens that explode and expand:
Shoes flash like fish as I tread the seas
And hang like fish when I stand,
And happiness swims in the shadow of trees
As the light blade hangs from my hand.

夜
の
酒
場 *IN THE BAR AT NIGHT*

In the bar at night
On its dark green wall
The hole appears,
Under the framed
Madonna shawled
In a trawl of tears.

As a magic button
Secret, a golden
Beetle wee,
The hole permits
The cold mosaiced
Eye to see

That strange far world,
That sesame-secret
Under-your-nose
Unknown world
That, close to knowing,
No one knows.

Even when drunk
And the glass ringing
Like a tolled bell,
The ghost so summoned
From that rum world

Will tell you nothing,
Proves infidel.

Even when drunk . . .
O doomed Madonna,
Suffer us stare
At the dark green wall
In the bar at night;
For the hole is there.

WOMAN

With lips light-pinkly painted
And powder smelling white
And cool about the neck-hair,
Woman, relax the tight
Thrust of your breasts against me,
Their sorbo surge. Be still,
And let your whitebait fingers
Their sly back-tickling skill,
Woman, forego. Abandon
Those surged and scented sighs
With which you now abandon
Yourself against my eyes.
Drop, woman, all your little tricks.
Woman, you're sad who know
That women, dupes of knowingness,
Can never let them go.

くさった蛤

ROTTEN CLAM

Over the naked poll
Of this dead mollusc stuck
Half-buried in the sand,
Its licking tongue a-loll,
Brine, gravel and sea-muck
Flow grating to and fro,
Flow without south or sound
As dreams to silence flow,
Slow-sluicingly.

Flickered through that dumb flux
The tongue's thin gabble glows
Red from the gravelly frot;
And when sad evening sucks
The sea down to expose
Wan flats where sadness broods,
From entrails on the rot
The putrid breath protrudes,
Flickeringly.

蝶
を
夢
む

TO DREAM OF A BUTTERFLY

The butterfly, small-faced and ugly-faced
With black long feelers, weightily let spread,
Like papers in the room, its large thick wings.
I came awake, and in my lone white bed
Quietly, quietly let the dream be traced
Back to its larva, its belittlings.

Back to that autumn where my griefs begin;
A lorn dusk saddened as the lights subside,
An old house rotting and crying tot,
The helpless soul of a small child that cried
Like some damp frog from grass run riot in
The rotting garden of a house on rot.

In that child's heart the most heart-rending things
Seemed to be soothed by those small lights that
    gloom
Edges of distant water; and I cried
Through long long hours of dream.
                              In some new room
A butterfly shakes out enormous wings,
Spreading, like papers, their thick whiteness wide.

肖
像 *PORTRAIT*

That creature with the sour
And always twisted face
Lurks in his hiding place
Close by the window-sill.

When white the cherries flower
Always, from some dark hole,
Some basement of the ground,
That creature, murk turned mole,
Comes cringingly around.

Over the window-sill,
Squirmed like an annelid,
He slid into my room
Who snapped him as he slid.

When in the reddish gloom
Of darkroom light I peered
As through a dripping sieve
At that pale negative,
Its ghostlinesses cleared
And slowly there appeared,
Like stains in a looking glass,
Something; a shadow-shape
Of some thing ominous.

Ah, from my neck and nape
Upwards, I found I was
Shaking like shiver-grass.

 WINTER

Symbols of sin appear in the sky.

Above the treetops and the blond
Snow-heaps, shining, they appear;
Mosaics of the atmosphere
Bright as if brazed to brightness by
A coldness burning far beyond
The mere mid-wintering of the year.

All see these symbols of your sin,
All read their shining sentence.

But mark the dark-as-Saladin,
The sleeping earth; and how therein
The simple creatures now begin
Building the house of your repentance.

春
夜　*SPRING NIGHT*

Dead hulls of life lie buried in the sands,
Of mussels maybe, sea-slugs, water-fleas:
And there, past numbering, emerge thin hands
Like threads of silk from nowhere; filigrees
Of thin thin groping hair that strains to be
By combers combed, sleeked out sea-wavily.

Rinsing the heart this lukewarm night of spring,
Indifferently, the brine-tide floods and flows
Over spent shells, the sadly flickering
Red tongues of mussels; stirs and shuffles those
Wracked seaward hankerings of tangled hair,
Those hands tressed out in dribbles of despair.

Stare down the far beach-distance. There
A line of legless cripples seems to creep
Over the wet waste, aimless; in whose hair,
Whose crimpled hair, the springnight spume hangs deep
While close and closer crawls, stump-stumblingly,
In lines of white-curled waves, the sexton sea.

あ
り
あ
け *DAWN*

From pain of long disease
The face is spider-webbed.
Below the waist the ebbed
Flesh had contracted to
Thin shadow-shapes, and these
Shaped shadows peter out
In nothings, in grey dream . . .

Above the waist there sprout
Things bushy, things that seem
Like brambles of bamboo.
The rotted hands are thin
And every piece and part,
Lips, knees and nails and heart,
Are smashed and battered in.

The moon is up today,
The day-moon's in the sky.
Its dawnly feeble ray,
Dim as a hand-lamp, glows
Weak as from over-load.
And somewhere far away,
Lifting its muzzle high,
A huge white dog gives tongue . . .

From desolation wrung,
Its desolation flows
Along the empty road,
Cry upon howling cry.

竹 *BAMBOOS*

Out of the shimmering earth
The bamboos grow, the green
Bamboos; and there, below,
Their growing roots grow lean
As thinlier they grow
Until their tiny tails,
A glitter of hairlets, make
Veined meshes, flimsy veils
Incredibly a-quake.

Out of the frozen earth
The bamboos grow, the tough
Intent bamboos that flow
Sky-tall with an almost rough
Interior rage to grow.
To grow. In hardening frost
Their knots swell hard with ooze.
To grow. The blue sky crossed
With growth, with green bamboos.

恋
を
恋
す
る
人

PERSON WHO LOVES LOVE

With crimsoned lips I kissed the trunk
Of a new white birch . . .
Yet even if I were a man of spunk
No breasts would lurch
Like rubber balls on my chest, and my
Slack skin would smell
Of no fine powder. But what am I
To be wishing me well?
A man in whom the sap ran dry,
A sherd, a shell.

But here on this fragrant summer's day,
In a sparkling grove's
Clearing I put myself away
And pull on gloves,
Gloves that over my whole hand slip
Like a sky sky-blue,
And a thing like a corset round my hip
I wrap on too,
And I fix my hair with a bobby-clip
As the young girls do.

I dust my neck with a sort of chalk
And I pat my hair,
Then, with that half-coquettish walk
And mincing air
Which girls affect, I tilt my head . . .
O pity me
As I kiss the trunk of the new white birch,
As I bend the knee,
As I cling, lips painted rosely red,
To that white tall tree.

有
害
な
る
動
物

HARMFUL ANIMALS

Things like dogs, by barking; by becoming
Deformed children, things like geese;
Things, by shining in the night, like foxes;
By congealing as crystal, things like tortoises;
And things like wolves that run as nothing can:
All these do harm to the good health of man.

白
い
月　*WHITE MOON*

Holding my cheek with toothache swollen,
I dug beneath a jujube tree,
Grubbying my delicate fingers,
Trying to sow, though seedily,
Some sort of seed.
                              Ah, I remember
As I was digging the frozen ground,
Cold in the dusk of that chill day,
Movement, slitherings; and I found
There at the bottom of the new-dug hole
An earthworm writhing.
                              So provoked,
From the low cover of a huddled house
The moon came sliding up. She stroked
The white ear of a woman. She
Came sliding up,
White,
Slitheringly.

悲しい月夜

SAD MOONLIT NIGHT

On the rotting wharf that pilfering cur,
Pale yapping waif of a wharfinger,
Barks at the moon:
The lonely at the lonelier.

O listen hard. By the wharf's stone wall
Where in the dark the water curls
To lap at land's ramshackledom,
There gloomy voices rise and fall,
Gloomy voices of yellow girls
Singing, singing of kingdoms come.

Why must I hear such singing; why
Must I be so ware of the world gone wry;
And why, pale dog,
Unhappy dog, am I always I?

海水旅館

SEASIDE HOTEL

As though afloat upon
The coast-woods of red pine
Far off, as far away
As shimmering can shine,
Somber, the combers shone.

How, bathed in that far glow,
Should one in passage pray?
How serve with hurried prayer
That shiningness, that slow
Sea-pulse which robes the bare
But bright-as-shoulderbone
Beaches of Echigo?

Finishing supper alone
In the underwater gloom
Of the hotel livingroom,
Suddenly things came right.

I rose; turned on the light.

野
鼠 *FIELDMOUSE*

Wherein consists our happiness?

The more one digs in muddy sand,
Will not one's grief well up the more
And one the more mistrust one's hand
As shiftiness grows yet more certain
And all the landmarks deliquesce?

Spring that swayed in the shadow of the curtain
Went jogging off like a rickishaw.

Where, o where, is our one true lover?
Though we stand in a field as wide as wind
And blow a whistle, we'll never recover
The day-dreamt girls. They will never come back.

And hopeless, honorless, scrubby-chinned,
In tear-stained togs like the sodden sack
That navvies wear, I walk benighted
Into my future's yesterday.

Remorse for things that can never be righted
Stirs like a fieldmouse, tweaks away.

酒精中毒者の死

DEATH OF AN ALCOHOLIC

From the dead body of the alcoholic
Lying on its back—slack mouth, sharp nose—
Around the area of the dead white stomach
Something unimaginable flows.

With blood congealed, translucent, blue;
Heart warped and many-angled;
With rotten guts and wrists frayed through
Rheumatically; with sticky tangled
Orts spread wetly everywhere;
The shining ground is bright.

The grass is sharp as shattered glass
And everything is shining
With radium's eerie light.

Landscape of despair,
Landscape with the moon declining.

Ah, in such a lonely place
The whitish murderer's hanging face
Laughs like a shimmer in the grass.

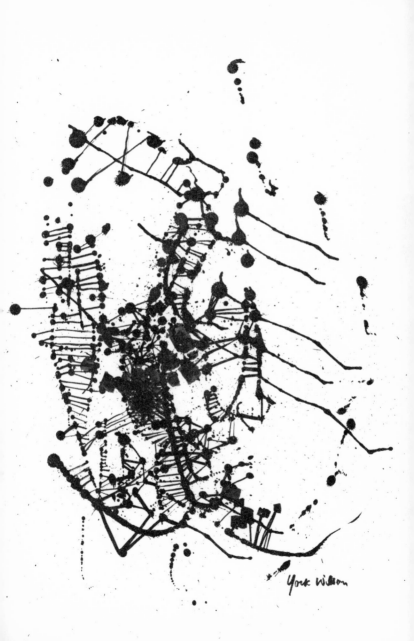

York Wilson

贈
物
に
そ
へ
て

WITH A GIFT

Some maybe so malign
Among the firing-party
As aimed but to decline
The bull's-eye of his heart.

Yet, when the magpied man,
Dead, to his dream-life drifted,
The skies with rancor ran.
This is that kind of gift.

卵　*EGGS*

High among twigs, light on their tiny tining,
The small eggs shine, halos on heaven's shelves:
And, looking up, we see the birds' nests shining
And know it time for easters of ourselves.

閑雅な食慾

ELEGANT APPETITE

Walking in a pine-wood
I came on a cafe.

Too far from town for visitors,
Tucked woodily away,
It was, as I remember it,
Both reticent and gay.

And there a girl whose manner wore
Love's shyness and its pride
Set out one plate as clean as day
And one bright fork beside
And brought, to shape my appetite,
An omelette and things fried.

The white clouds floated overhead,
And still their shadows shine
As I remember elegance,
As I sit down to dine
Who know there's now no appetite
More elegant than mine.

艶めかしい墓場

ENCHANTEN GRAVEYARD

From the direction of the viewing-stand
Come faintly tepid, stanked saltwater smells.
The willows shimmy in the wind. Where else,
As slugs crawl up, black gland on glistening gland,
The moon-sharp hedge, could such a dumping-
    ground,
So gloom-engorged a cemetery be found?

O strange girl-shadow, green and delicate,
Pale green, a mouldering of the atmosphere,
For what wan purpose are you wandered here,
Who are not shellfish, pheasant, even cat,
The common kindred of this sullen coast,
But a mere lonely, a most lonely, ghost?

From the green shadow of your drifting mort
Drift smells of rotten fish, the stink of one
Whose guts have melted pulpy in the sun
On some backstreet in some poor fishing-port:
Sad wrenching smell, and vile beyond all wrench,
The smell of grief; unbearable sorrow's stench.

What is it, then, you are who, this spring night
As spring night tepid, tenuously go
Mild as a younger sister, kimono
Trailing its charmed bright crimson? It is not

The graveyard's moonlight, phosphorescences,
Shadow or truth. But just how sad it is.

Only how sad it is. For thus and thus
My life and body, clammy as wet clay,
To meld with yours rot clammily away.
The veils of putrefaction smoke for us;
And into nothingness, that vague morass,
My being slithers from its last Alas.

龜　*TURTLE*

Woods, swamps and the cobalt
Sky-carapace, sky-vault.

Heavy to human hands
The pure gold turtle sleeps
Whose quiet shining weight
Weighs on the mind more deeply
The more one thinks and thinks
Of quietude innate,
The more one understands
Man's animal estate.

And down the sky's blue deeps,
Shining, the turtle sinks.

天
景　*SKYSCAPE*

Go, gently creaking cart.

The sea shimmers towards brightness. Wheat,
Towards some infinitely distant part,
Into the distance ripples its retreat.

Go gently, creaking cart.

And through a skyscape shining, through
The birds and fishes shining at its heart,
Beyond the building windowed blue,

Go, gently creaking, cart.

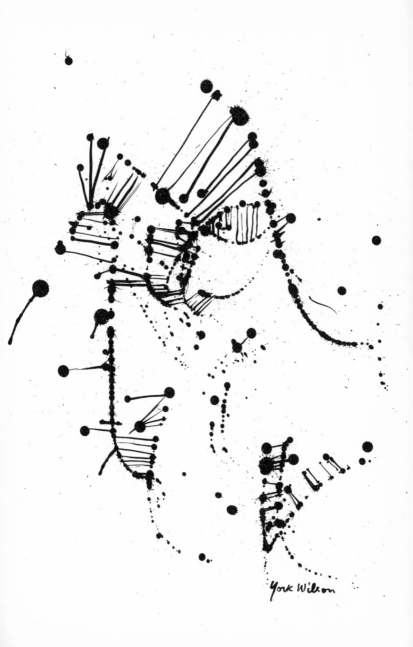
York Wilson

地面の底の病気の顔

FACE AT THE BOTTOM
OF THE WORLD

Face at the bottom of the world:
A sick, a lonely face,
One invalided out
Of every inner place;
Yet, slowly there uncurled,
Green in the gloom the grasses sprout.

And, as a rat's nest stirs,
Its million tangled hairs
One queasy quivering,
Thinnest of winterers,
The bamboo shoot prepares
Its green grope to the spring.

Sad in the ailing earth,
Tongue-tender with despair,
Green moves through grief's grimace;
And, sick and lonely, there
In the gloom of the under world,
At the bottom of the world, a face.

BLUE FLAME

Look, all sins are written down;
But not all sins were mine.

Truly what appeared to me
Was no more than the shine,
The sallow flat reflection
Of a shadowless blue flame,
Merely a ghost of feelings
Too flimsy for a name
Which disappeared on wastes of snow.

How then should I express
Repentance, real and suffocating
As man's remorselessness,
For days of such slight pressure?
How should I grapple shame,
When sin is but a shadow
Of that shadowless blue flame?

小出新道

NEW ROAD AT KOIDE

This road, just newly opened, goes
Straight to the city, I suppose.
  Dark melancholy day.
I stand at a new crossing where
A new horizon like a tear
    Runs lonelily away.

The sun above a straggling row
Of huddled roof-tops huddles low . . .
  How thin, how shorn of shade,
Stand the few trees in that sparse wood
That once so greenly sturdy stood
    Before the road was made.

Such bleakness feeds my blemished mood
Of anger and incertitude
  As black sorts well with black.
How, how can I re-fangle me?
How be what once I used to be?
    Where does the road run back?

O where's that leafy road I seek
That runs to boyhood from the bleak
  Horizons of the town?
For this new road, which I reject
And will not travel, more was wrecked
    Than all those trees hacked down.

月光と海月

MOONLIGHT AND JELLYFISH

I swim in the moonlight, swim to snare
Jellyfish swarming, flocks of phlegm.

My hands stream out, forgoing me:
Further and further they extend
Among those moving mirrors where,
Coiling, the seaweeds cumber them;
Where, in the mooned alembic sea,
My flesh turns glassy, glassily.

A thing transparent, a chilly thing,
Flows in the water, knows no end . . .

My soul, near frozen, shivering,
Sinks in the sea, is almost drowned,
Drowned in its very trance of prayer
While, swarming everywhere around,
Swarming around me everywhere,
The jellyfish in trembles of pure blue
Swim out, swim through
That moonlight they are turning to . . .

お
よ
ぐ
ひ
と

SWIMMER

The swimmer's skin diagonals the water,
His hands stretch out together as in prayer;
His heart, as any jellyfish translucent,
Shines in the water and is water there.

The swimmer's eyes are listening through water
To the drowned promise of a hanging bell;
His soul observes the white moon on the water.
There is but water in a wishing well.

貝 *SEA SHELL*

A thing most cold is born; its teeth
Flow in the water, and its hands
Flow in the water underneath
Things colder than it understands.

Though on the tide's wide spread and sprawl
It drifts to distance, still, if I,
Treading in shallow water, call,
Its very distance will reply.

珈
琲
店
酔
月

CAFE OF THE DRUNKEN MOON

Unable to stand my thirst,
I cope with the little slope
But stagger as I open
The door of the Drunken Moon.

Out of the shambled shop
The spinning noises burst
As from a burnt balloon;
And broken records blast
With ricochets of song
The sooted lamps, the slop
And that poor bottle-show
Of drab suburban spirit
A-jitter in a row.

How long, my heart, how long
Must this dark sorrow last?

Now, homeless, I am grown
Drunken and old and grey
And desperately alone.
My wife and children went
Somewhere. I could not say
Where, but they went away;
And I am on my own
With leisure to repent,

To drift from day to day,
Drift and be desolate.

Under the leaning wall
Women, how many, many
Around the table crowd
Who, seeing my drunken state,
First pitied me aloud
But, in no time at all,
Name-calling in their blatant
Straight brawling over prey,
Snatched up my purse and then
Counted its piddling yen
Down to the last thin penny,
Stole them; and went away.

 STILL LIFE

The heart of this still life is deeply angry,
Its surface grieves too deeply to be told:
Reflected in the white eyes of this vessel,
The cold greens near the window are twice cold.

磨かれたる金属の手

POLISHED METAL HANDS

My hands are magnet. Look, they are
Platinum, and rheumatism's
Rink of pain.
They glimmer in the heart of trees,
In fish, in tombstones; there they glimmer
Half-right as rain.

Already from the limbs they drift
Burning hot, already frantic,
Drifting away . . .
The fingers open, groping after
Revelation. The hands glimmer
In the dead of day:

In the dead center of all creation
My hands glimmer, my polished metal
Glimmering hands.
They blind my eyes, they rip my flesh,
They damage bone. A terrible, terrible
Glimmer of hands.

My hands are a white, a rotted radium
And my fingers hurt
Violently. O they hurt
So hard I secretly swallow this needle
Honed for the heart.

盆
景 *DWARF LANDSCAPE*

Spring and summer have both waned away.
The hands, the hands are amber;
Amber the maple-leaf.

Wet as a water-tray
The eye reflects September
Where, hazy under water,
Stones of hazy green
Secrete the smell of grief.

Look, deep in that mountain waterscape,
Slim as a silver wish,
A waterfall from water
Runs shivering to shape
The first white nerve of winter.

Look, in that shriveled scene
A waterfall from water,
Blenched by its own escape,
Runs cold and shiverish.

And coldly through the water,
Stone-coldly, sink the fish.

晚
秋　*LATE AUTUMN*

A train was passing overhead.
My random thoughts were shadewards led
And, looking back, I was surprised
To find my heart so tranquilized.

Along the autumn streets were strewn
The last rays of the afternoon,
And traffic thronged the thoroughfare.
Do I exist? Is there-ness there?

Yet in a house, a gone-for-broke
House on a backstreet where the smoke
Still hangs in shreds, a window blocks
Its hollowness with hollyhocks.

York Wilson

夜
汽
車 *NIGHT TRAIN*

In daybreak's feeble light
The fingerprints that sour
The glass of the sliding door
Glint desolately chill.
Rock-ridges, barely white,
Are still, quicksilver still.

No passengers yet wake.
The fagged electric light
Sighs wearily. The sweet,
The too-sweet varnish-smell
And my cigar's stale smoke
Have made the morning vile.

Yet, if it seems to me
Vile, how much filthier
It must appear to her,
That wife of someone, met
Merely by rail-chance.
                    Haven't we
Passed Yamashina yet?

She turns her pillow's vent
Watching with woman's eyes
Until the cushion sighs
As winded babies do . . .

In sudden grief we leant
Closer and closer to

And, so companioned,
We watched beyond the pane
Of that drab railway train
The landscape gorge the light;
And columbines, beyond
Some village wall, were white.

蛙
の
死 *DEATH OF A FROG*

Where the frog was smashed
The children stood,
Stood in a circle
Unabashed
And unamazed,
Their hands upraised
Together, good.

Bloody and sweet
In that ringed place,
They placed their hands
On the moon's fat O.
And someone stands
On a hill; a hat
And a face below.

殺
人
事
件

MURDER CASE

There sounds a shot of pistol
In the faraway sky; and then
A pistol-shot again.

Two pistol-shots; and my
Detective dressed in glass
Warps in from that clear sky,
Vitrescent but to find
Behind the window pane
He takes such pains to pass
The floorboards cut from crystal.

Between the fingers wind
Ribbons of blood more blue
Than words for blue contain,
And from the glazen dew
That glints like cellophane
On that sad woman's corpse
A chill, chill cricket chirps.

One morning of an early
November, dressed in glass,
The sad detective, surly
From sadnesses, came down
And, where the two roads cross
To quatrify the town,

Turned. At his point of turning
An autumn fountain waited.

Already isolated
In knowingness, he only
Can feel the real bereavement,
The long slow wrench concerning
Identity's decay.

Look, on the distant lonely
Acres of marble pavement
The villain, quick as silver,
Glides silverly away.

山
居   *IN THE MOUNTAINS*

October, at the fading of the year,
Waits for my prayers and silences.
The birds and fishes disappear
Into their fasting distances
And autumn flowers fade. Their colors seep
To lend the whitening air an opal shine.
Nothing, not even prayer, dare run too deep.
Touch but a Bible, it turns argentine.

INDEX OF TITLES